I0476154

Get yourself Debt Free!

Change The Way You Think About Debt To Dig Your Way Out

Pierre Romberger

Legal & Disclaimer

The author has made every effort to ensure the accuracy of the information within this book was correct at time of publication. The author does not assume and hereby disclaims any liability to any party for any loss, damage, or disruption caused by errors or omissions, whether such errors or omissions result from accident, negligence, or any other cause.

Introduction

If you are like lots of people, where your debts get in the way of your dreams. In this book, we will lay out a strategy to get you well on your way to becoming debt-free.

This will not happen overnight. You must commit yourself to tracking spending and cutting it, where needed, so that you can pay down your debt. This may mean making some changes in your lifestyle.

After you target your debt, use the steps in this book to list the debts as you will be paying off, and list your other money spent, so you know where you need to make cuts.

Each time you reach a repayment milestone, don't be afraid to celebrate. This will motivate you to keep going, and your progress will become more tangible. Being debt free will give you more freedom than you can possibly imagine. Read on to learn how to make that dream a reality.

Chapter 1

Don't be Ashamed of Debt – Speak to Someone about it

Among your family and friends, there is probably one person you can speak with about almost anything. You know, someone who's really close to you. She can help you climb out of your debt by helping you set targets and then attain them.

Not everyone will be OK with talking about money matters. Some friends are not comfortable with it. Find one who will be there for you, to listen to you about your debt problem.

Being in debt is not a good feeling. Your friend will understand how you feel in this kind of situation, especially if she's been through it herself. Getting out of debt isn't an easy journey, but if you have perseverance and someone to talk with about the process, you can be debt-free. People often feel shame when they tell friends about financial difficulties. It's mainly because they feel ashamed. You shouldn't feel this way.

Tell your Friend the Whole Story

Open up and tell your friend all the details of your debt issues. She can help you much more easily if she knows as much as you're willing to tell her about what happened that plunged you into debt. If she is going to offer you valuable advice, she should know as much as she can about the problem.

Your close friend can spend time with you when you're down in the dumps. There are ways you can spend time together without spending a lot of money. If she finds things to do that aren't expensive, she can be a valuable role model for you, too.

Debt Counseling

If your friend has been in debt before, she may recommend that you go to debt counseling. Counselors are trained in all kinds of areas, like consumer rights, collections, debt management and budgeting.

Financial counselors will spend about a half hour with you, and evaluate the information you're sharing with them. You'll learn the positives and minuses of plans for debt management. Your own plan will be tailored just for your financial needs, to help you get out of debt for good.

Talk to your friend about finding a good debt counselor to talk to. You can talk to someone on the phone, in person or even online. Some counselors offer low cost or free services. Check the Better Business Bureau to make sure your choice is a good one.

Allow your Friend to help you through the Process

As you break down the issues that led to your debt, talk to your friend about helping you set realistic goals. She will be there to support you along the way, and give you a pat on the back when you reach a target.

Chapter 2

It's not OK to be in Debt – Changing your Mindset

Shopping is fine, right? If you want something and you work hard, you should have it, right? Wrong! It's not OK if it puts you in deeper debt. It's not OK to be in debt.

Even if you've been in debt for a long time, you might still not remember all the issues that led to your problem. If you like to spend money when you're feeling blue, this is something you can talk over with your friend. She can suggest different ways to brighten your mood without spending a lot of money.

Buying Things to Feel Good

Lots of people buy things they think will make them feel better, but those feelings won't last for long when you take a look at your bills again. Lots of people have high balances on their credit cards, so you're surely not alone. That doesn't mean it's OK to blow money when you're feeling down. You'll worry even more about your debt if you do.

Everyone has hobbies, but shopping is not a hobby. If you buy things on impulse, you may run up a lot of debt in a short time. If you can't afford all the things you buy, you may even have to sell some of them to pay bills.

Keep Track of your Purchases

Buying things whenever you're in the mood to buy makes it harder to track all of your expenses. If you buy things just for good feelings, you'll have a greater chance of falling into debt. It may not be the only reason, but it could be a big one. When you have maxed out your credit cards and you owe people money, it's a bad thing.

Managing Non-Essential Expenses

You need to learn to manage the ways you spend money, or you'll never get out of debt. You will always have to pay bills like your mortgage and utilities, and if you cut back on buying things you don't need, it'll be easier to pay those regular bills.

Some people live in debt for most of their adult lives. College debt or mortgage debt are parts of life, but getting out of debt is a rewarding path, and you'll be glad you took it. When you're in debt, you'll be stressed out financially and emotionally. Set up a plan to get yourself out of debt and then stick to it.

Now that you're in debt, planning to get out will help you in learning lots of useful skills in money management. When you work hard and pay off a sizable chunk of debt, you'll feel better and you will be way better off.

If you're still young and in debt, you may not have as many financial responsibilities, so it could be easier to dig your way out. It's a lot more stressful to be in debt if you have a spouse and family. They depend on you.

It's just another Goal

You don't have to allow your debt to leave you

feeling worried and weary all the time. When you make solid plans to get out of debt AND follow them, you'll feel much more relaxed, and even liberated.

Life throws you curve balls sometimes, so you may have to adjust parts of your debt payment plan. This is OK, but you still need to keep your eye on the prize, which is being debt-free.

Chapter 3

What you Want versus what you Need

We live in a world of instant gratification. If you want something, it's way too easy to go online and buy it with a couple clicks. This just digs you more deeply into debt, if your money should be targeted to bills and you don't have extra money to play with. You may feel guilty about the purchase, and talk yourself into believing that something you want is actually something you need.

It's time for you to grow up financially, and spend wisely on the things you need. You're not alone, either. Lots of people look like adults but spend money like children on things they want. You need to learn how to distinguish things you want from things you need, so that your plan to become debt-free will work for you.

Necessary Needs

You do need some things to stay alive. This includes water, food and shelter. Without these, you can't survive. There is no specific type of shelter you must have. You don't have to live in an expensive house or apartment.

Needs that are Less Necessary

If you have a job, you probably need a dependable vehicle to get there. This is not a have-to, though. You can use public transportation, carpool or ride a bike if you have to. That doesn't have to be a permanent thing, but it can certainly save you a lot of money.

Your job will also determine the types of clothing you need. Business and professional workers may need suits, while blue collar workers can get by with well-made clothes that are not necessarily stylish.

Wants versus Needs

Everything else is simply a want. Nothing else is a need. There are many levels of things you want.

Some wants are a lot closer to needs than others. For example, if you have a computer that's not dead, then you don't need a new one. If it dies, you can still use one at the library or local school, until you can afford to buy a new one.

However, you would benefit from a new computer. It would be much faster, so that you could get your work done sooner. It wouldn't be as likely to crash, so the work you do will be safer. So, maybe a computer is almost a need for you. New pairs of boots, on the other hand, are probably not.

It can be hard to think this way. It can take weeks or months before you can readily define wants and needs. You have to be ruthless, and be truthful with yourself, no matter how much you want something. You have to learn to say NO to yourself.

In our world of advertisements, people seem to be telling you that they have something you need, but that's often not the case at all. You have to evaluate what you are seeing and hearing, and be honest about what you need and what you only want.

"Wants" and Happiness

Are you happier when you decide to buy things you want? Not really. Focusing on what you want makes you feel deprived. The definition of something you want is something you don't have, and you'll never be fulfilled if you're always focusing on what you don't have. Be grateful for the things you have, instead.

Once people make a lot of money, are they happier? Actually, studies show that happiness does not increase with your income level. Is that surprising? Not really. Once you have the things you need, and have money set aside for emergencies and your retirement, your happiness level is fairly set.

In our materialistic society, you can become preoccupied with gaining more wealth or more possessions. Earning a high salary feels good, and it's not morally wrong, but the fat bank account won't make you any happier, in truth.

Fulfilling your needs makes you happy. Fulfilling your wants does not. Focus on what is enough for your needs, and your life will be more balanced. The less you spend on wants, the easier it is to get out of debt.

When you examine yourself and your life, you need clarity on what you really need, so that you can keep it separate from what you want. Keep your "wants" in check and work towards fulfilling your needs.

Is more better? Not if you're honest with yourself. Debt is the result of pursuing more than you can have based on what you make. It's natural for you to want more good things – it's human. But it can confuse you and lead you off course. There are limits to meeting your personal needs, and you must keep that in mind, or your journey out of debt will take a lot longer.

Chapter 4

Successful Ways to Pay off Debt

If your to-do list every month includes paying a huge chunk of change on your credit cards and other debts, you are not alone. About 40% of Americans have high credit card debt. The average is about $4,800 in total debt just on credit cards.

You will have to change your spending habits if you don't have enough money left each month to make a dent in your debt. Here are some strategies that will help.

High Interest Payoff

One method has you focus on the debts that have the highest interest rates. Attacking them first will save you more in interest fees. This makes sense, since the largest debts usually cause you the most pain. If you only pay a minimum amount every month, you're only going deeper into debt.

Focus on those high-interest debt payments, while you still make minimum payments on debts with lower balances and interest rates. Once you pay off one debt, hit the next one with the highest balance, until you've eliminated your debt.

You should know up-front that this is a slow approach. Even though it's a good plan, it will take time. If you have yourself buried in debt, and you live from paycheck to paycheck, you may be overwhelmed by how slowly you are paying things off. Don't fall off the wagon and use credit cards that add more debt to the picture.

This method works better if you behave more on the numbers basis, rather than emotionally. It is useful if it will take years to pay off your high interest debts. If your interest rates are relatively low, this method may not be your best bet.

Plan Two – Hit Debts with Low Balances

If you need to see progress, hit debts with low

balances, and pay them off. After you have done that, then take on those high interest and high balance debts. The extra money in this plan snowballs, so that you can overpower the debt more quickly.

This method won't save you as much money on interest, but it is psychologically helpful. Seeing a debt with a zero balance is uplifting, as long as you don't start using credit cards you have paid off, again.

Which Plan will Work Best for You?

So which one is better, paying off the higher debts first or paying off the smallest debts so that they're out of the way? There are pluses to both methods.

If you're helped by positive emotions, paying off lower debts first may be better for you. We mentioned this approach above, and it involves paying off smaller debts first. This provides you with victories you can use to keep motivated to dig your way out of debt.

What about Emergencies?

While you're concentrating on paying off your debt, you still need to set aside money for emergencies. Don't rely on credit cards you've paid off as your sources for emergency funds. If you do, you'll end up in the same hole of debt if something unexpected demands money.

Rebuilding your Credit Score

Are you concerned about your credit score? If you have high debt, you should be. Tackling debts that are close to their credit line will open up your available credit, and this will boost your credit score. As you pay debts down, you'll have a higher amount of credit available, and this is one of the main ways the credit bureaus use in determining your overall credit score.

Chapter 5

Do your own Balance Sheet - Income versus Spending

The best way to know your starting point in debt is by doing your own balance sheet. This will calculate your net worth by comparing what you own with what you owe. The difference between them is your net worth. Don't be too discouraged if your net worth comes up negative. Setting goals is easier if you know right where you stand.

Your assets will include lots more than just your investments and house, and your liabilities go beyond your mortgage and other debts.

To do your personal balance sheet, gather all your financial information. List your assets with their values, the cash you have either in CDs, bank accounts or money market accounts, investments and the value of your home and car. Add in the value of your personal property and any other assets you own.

Now figure out your total liabilities. This includes the remaining balance on your mortgage, auto loans, personal loans, student loans and the balances on your credit cards. The sum of monies you owe is your total liability. When you start digging your way out of debt, it will decrease your liabilities.

The difference between total assets and total liabilities will be your net worth. Paying down your debt will help the balance to tip in your favor.

Include these Assets

If you're employed and under 50 years of age, your paycheck is a valuable asset. This should influence the way you handle your finances. You'll need disability, health and life insurance. This will help your family to cope if your income is lost.

Your paycheck also allows you to invest in stocks, when you are still young. If you don't save enough through your working years, you can work after retirement age, at least part time, to increase your assets. Social security is also part of your assets as you age, and the benefits could amount to almost half of your total wealth, assuming the plan is still solvent when you retire.

Social security will generate income that increases with inflation. If your employer offers you a pension, too, that will add to your net worth.

Other Financial Obligations

Your liabilities include saving for your retirement and the time when you will no longer be working. Your family can be considered an obligation, but they can also provide a safety net, if you fall on hard times and need to borrow money.

The Overall View

Your personal balance sheet will help you watch your spending while you increase your net worth. They aren't just charts or graphs; they help you take a good look at where your money goes and how you can cut back on spending by paying off debt.

If you find positive cash flow one month, use that money to pay on your debt. This will help open the door for increasing assets without also increasing you liabilities.

The Bottom Line

If you're deep in debt, your cash flow may be in the negative most months. Take a good hard look at your spending habits and make adjustments that will help. Using balance sheets will keep you more aware of the ways you spend money, and allow you to watch your liabilities become smaller, as you pay off your debt.

Chapter 6

Budget, Budget, Budget – Know where you stand

Nothing is more important to getting out of debt than setting up a realistic budget. What goals do you have, financially? What debts do you have to pay? Making a budget involves some tough choices, but your goals will make budgeting less painful, and you'll have a better handle on the debt you still owe.

Where is your money coming from?

Your budget starts out with listing your income sources. This includes work, money from student loans, etc. Keep totals of how much you make from each source each month.

Where is your money going?

When you look at your bank account at the end of each month, do you wonder where it all went? You have to know how you spend your money. Track your expenses on a spreadsheet for a month so you know where your money goes.

You can separate your living expenses into categories:

Fixed Needs – These stay the same every month and include rent or mortgage, utilities, etc.

Variable Needs –These are also necessary, but the amounts vary each month. They include food and gas.

Wants – We've talked about these. They include non-essential things like a new smartphone, eating out and going to movies.

Putting your expenses into categories helps you budget your money, and that will help you pay down your debt. If you save money every month, include that in your expenses. Plan your savings. If you have unforeseen expenses, you should be able to pay for them without digging yourself further into debt. If you don't need the money for emergencies, you can save it to follow dreams in your future.

Adding Everything up

In comparing your income and your expenses, you should have enough money to handle the bills. If your expenses are higher than your income, you'll need to make adjustments. These include spending less on the "Wants" you have listed above.

Note any large expenses that pop up every month. If you spend a lot on non-essentials, you need to tighten the budget. Set limits for your wants, so that you won't go over the amounts and ruin your budget. If you can get by without monthly spending on electronics or clothing, this will help you to free up money to pay down your debt.

If you're unable to trim some money from your "wants" list, you will have to reduce other expenditures. This could mean taking public transportation or carpooling for awhile instead of driving, and maybe even downsizing to a smaller home.

Once you have found a way to keep up with

your budgeting, you'll be better able to see where the money should be going, as opposed to where it is going.

Chapter 7

Always Pay Yourself First, before others

If you're like lots of people in debt, you may tell yourself you'll start saving for retirement NEXT month. Your money seems targeted to bills and debt right now.

The problem here is obvious, isn't it? After you pay all your monthly bills including payments on debts, you don't have money left to save, until your next paycheck. And then the same thing happens with that check, too. Maybe you eat out a few too many times or maybe you found a great price on a motorcycle. Those things won't help you in retirement or in an emergency.

Pay yourself First

Paying yourself first means putting away money for savings before you pay your debt down. Set aside some of your income each payday, before you spend money on discretionary things. If you're like most people, you'll only try to save what money you have left over, and that may be zero in many months. That's paying yourself last.

When you pay yourself first, you ensure that you will be able to cover your financial goals in the future. This includes contributing money towards your retirement, and setting aside money for emergencies. You should cover those bases before you spend money on things you want now, like a night out with friends.

This means that you have to set your mind to pay yourself first. This can be challenging for even money-savvy people, so it's something you'll always have to keep in mind when you are paid.

Why should you pay yourself now?

Paying yourself first has been promoted and talked about for many years, but most people just don't do it. Many people don't have any emergency savings, and if you spend all your money when you're paid, this includes you.

Your nest egg is important, too. Social Security is facing shortfalls already, and you don't want to be stuck after you retire, having to work for years to make up for that. It's not fair, but those are the facts. If your company doesn't have a pension plan, you should also be paying yourself by putting money into a 401-K or other retirement plan. This is your responsibility.

If you're in debt, those payments are just that much more money you won't use to pay yourself. As important as paying down debt is, paying yourself still should come first. The cost of living is high, and your day to day expenses make it harder to pay yourself.

The sooner you start paying yourself first, the better off you will be in the future. You can take advantage of the interest that helps your money grow more quickly, and you'll also ensure that financial goals are being funded before life steps in with another curve ball. If you wait too long, you may have a major auto repair, a large medical bill or a layoff, and any of these will throw your goals off track.

Bills should not be surprising, but there are always things happening that you can't control. If you don't have emergency savings, you'll be forced to turn to credit cards, payday lenders (gasp!) or your family to pay those bills.

A note here about payday lenders: DON'T use them. They charge interest rates in the hundreds of percentage points and you'll end up paying a whole lot more than you borrowed.

Setting and forgetting your Savings

If you always pay your bills first and then check to see what you have left, it may be hard for you to train yourself to make "you" the first person you pay. It challenges the way you've always handled your bills, and it means you'll need to spend less on things you want, or you'll never have money put aside for the time you need it.

Prioritize your Future

When you look at a list of your debts, you may think it's unrealistic to think about paying yourself before you pay your bills. Although you must pay bills on time, you also need to plan for your future. It can't always take a back seat to your monthly commitments. Here are some steps that will make it easier to pay yourself first:

1.   Determine how much you can afford. Look closely at your expenses, and see where you can make changes in your spending, like taking a sack lunch to work or getting your hair cut at a beauty school instead of an expensive salon. These are not large amounts initially, but they can really add up over time.

2.   Create a strategy for savings. Once you find the money to use in paying yourself, determine a good way to save these funds until you need them. Moving money into your savings account when you're paid is a good way to set it aside. You can split your employer's direct deposit plan to send some to savings instead of checking. That makes it harder to spend.

You could also set up an automatic funds transfer each payday, sending money from checking to savings. This will help you in getting used to managing your day to day expenses with a smaller paycheck.

You can set up new plans or cancel money transfers when you need to, but it's important to remain consistent and treat this money you're saving as off-limits unless you have an emergency.

3. Set up a goal for personal payment. If you have determined that you can only pay yourself a small dollar amount now, look for chances to increase those payments in the future, as your debts are paid off. How much of your salary do you need to set aside to meet financial goals, like saving for college or retirement? Make changes in the way you spend money that will have a positive impact on your expenses, long-term.

You may find out, for example, that you don't need all those premium channels on your cable plan, so update it and set aside the difference in your savings account.

You probably won't see an immediate benefit to paying yourself first. Don't be discouraged. If you have a financial emergency, this strategy will help you through that storm. Paying yourself first depends on your willingness to put yourself first. This money helps to prepare you for whatever may happen in the future.

Chapter 8

Always Pay your Bills on Time
–
Save Money on Late Fees

When you can reliably pay your bills on time, this is an important way you are taking control of your finances. You need to remember when bills are due and pay them on time. This not only reduces stress, but it also boosts your credit score and saves you money, since you won't be paying extra money in late fees.

Start a Habit of Paying Bills on-time

1.   Use financial software to remind you of automatic bill payments. Quicken and Microsoft Money both have special features that will prompt you weeks or days before your bills are due.

2.   Set up automatic payments. Most regular bills, like mortgages, utilities and auto loans give you

an option of having money taken automatically from your account when the bills are due. This makes it impossible to forget. A note, though: if you have payments taken from a debit card and your bank or credit union sends you a new card every couple of years, contact those creditors and update your debit card on file.

3. Learn your billing cycle. Review a few months of paid bills and list your bills in the order that they come due. You'll probably notice that the bill due dates will either be closer to the beginning or end of each month. Pay the bills due before you next paycheck as soon as you are paid (after putting money aside for yourself).

If you don't have the funds to make all the payments early in the month, contact a few creditors and have them bump your payment date to one later in the month.

4. Organize your bills. Your bills need to be arranged by due date. Mark them on your calendar if you have no other way to remind yourself. If you still get paper bills in the mail, note the due date and

highlight it as soon as you open it. A desk file will allow you to sort bills by due dates. This is a visual reminder of what bill needs to be paid next.

5. Prepay your bills. If it's a problem for you to pay bills on time, you can prepay them to avoid late fees. If you have a paycheck with a lot of overtime on it, use it to prepay some bills. Mark the bills as paid so that you don't forget you've already paid them.

6. Consolidate your bills. If you get your cable, phone and internet services from one company, have them put the amounts in one bill. This makes it less likely that you'll miss a due date. It will also save you a few bucks in postage over the course of a year, if you still mail your payments.

7. Sign up for bills and reminders in your email. You probably check your email multiple times a day. Use your creditors' online bill payment reminders. An even better choice is going "paperless". This means your bill will be sent right to your email address. As soon as you receive the email bill, log into your account and pay it, if funds allow for it, so you won't miss due dates.

8. If you still get paper bills, create a place to pay bills. When you pick up your mail, be sure you don't lay it down somewhere or stick it into a purse, where it could be forgotten. Keep your bills in one place, where you write checks. If you pay your bills online, keep them close to your computer.

9. Schedule a time to pay bills. Set aside time to pay your bills regularly. Make it just like any other event that you put on your schedule. When you set aside regular bill-paying days, you are less likely to miss any due dates.

10. Give your check time to get to your creditor. If you still pay by snail mail, make sure you send the payment so that it has sufficient time to arrive before it will be considered late. Try to meet or beat deadlines, rather than missing them by one or two days. Every late fee adds up.

11. Pay bills by phone. Many of your creditors will allow you to pay your bills with your phone. There may be a small fee for this. If you find yourself paying late fees all the time, paying by phone may be cheaper than paying late fees. It will certainly look better on

your payment record.

Why does it Matter?

Paying your bills before the due date does matter. It will help you establish a better credit record. When you pay on time, your creditors report prompt payments to the credit bureaus. The better your credit record, the more likely you will be to get credit in the future, and at better rates.

Paying bills on time saves money, too. You won't be paying penalties or late fees. On credit cards, for example, the creditor can raise your interest rate if you pay their bills late. This can even happen after just one late payment.

A Big Payoff in Small Steps

Paying bills on time will help to reduce financial stress. You won't have to wonder if you forgot a bill, since you will know they have all been paid. Choose one or two of the tips above and incorporate as many as you need to make paying bills on time a habit.

Chapter 9

Reduce your Expenses – Make it Possible to Pay off Debt

The biggest challenge in your financial situation is to figure out ways where you can spend less money. Cutting down on expenses is the best way to accomplish this. Even small bills add up, and they all drain your resources.

Look for ways to cut your expenses that are easily implemented and also effective. Here are some ways to can save money on your routine expenses.

Ways to Save on Debt

If you can reduce the amount of money you owe, you can lower monthly expenses. Paying down debt, which is the goal of this e-book, means you'll have fewer bills to pay every month. This will free up more of your paycheck. Here are some ways to cut down on your debt, to save money and reduce your expenses.

1. Consolidate Student Loans

Some student loans have high interest rates. Can you consolidate some or all of these loans? A good consolidation plan could leave you with extra cash every month.

2. Refinance your Car or Home

If there is a chance to refinance your car or house, ask at your lending institutions. Even if you are underwater in your current mortgage, you may be able to refinance with the HARP program. If you lock in a lower rate, it can reduce your monthly bills and save you money in the long run, too.

3. Request a Reduction in Credit Card Rates

If you have large balances on credit cards, call the companies and ask if they will grant you a reduction in your interest rate. They may negotiate if you pay your bills on time. Be sure you don't use your credit cards all the time, since that will build your debt back up.

4. Try Balance Transfers

If some of your debt has high interest rates, balance transfers may be good options. The best cards offer 0% APR for a year or so. A 0% APR will help you pay your debt down more quickly, and save interest money. There may be fees associated with balance transfers, so check on them.

5. Sell Items you don't Need

Look through your attic or closets for things you don't use anymore. If they have value, list them on Craigslist or eBay. You can use that money to help in paying off debt.

6. Sign up for Automatic Billing Plans

Many instalment loan plans, especially student loans, will offer you a reduction in your interest rate if you set up automatic billing. Don't pass these offers by. They reduce your monthly expenses and they're also convenient, ensuring that you won't miss any payments.

Ways to Cut your Insurance Expense

Everyone needs insurance, to protect against unexpected occurrences. Here are some options on reducing insurance premiums.

1. Raise Deductibles

If you have a small deductible, you're paying a larger premium. You could switch that, particularly if you don't have frequent claims. Raising the deductible on your policies can reduce your premiums, which reduces your insurance costs.

2. Look into Term Life Insurance

If you have universal or whole life insurance, look at term policies. The cost will be less, even if the coverage is similar. The big difference? Your term coverage will terminate at a certain time, usually after you have retired. By that time, your family won't be as dependent on you.

3. Shop for Cheaper Auto or Homeowners Insurance or Bundle them

If your credit is still fairly good, you might want to look into cheaper insurance on your car and your home. You may be able to maintain your current coverage level and reduce your expenses by going to another company. If you get a good quote from a new company, give your existing company a chance to match it before you switch.

If you bundle your auto and homeowners insurance together, you will usually get a nice discount. If you have two different insurance companies now, ask both about discounts available if you bundle your policies.

4. Downgrade Health Insurance

Check with your employer to see if there is a way to reduce your cost for insurance. Be sure to keep your family covered, as well as yourself. Consider a higher deductible, especially if you don't have serious health issues or regular prescriptions. Be sure that your expected savings will outweigh any increases in out of pocket costs.

Saving Money on Food

Food is one area where you may frequently go over your budget. Families eat a lot, and eat out, and this impacts your expenses. Here are a few ways you can save on food.

1. Buy Generic Brands

Many foods (and other products) are available in a generic or store brand at lower prices. Check the ingredients and if they are similar, the taste will likely be similar, too. Try generic brands once to give them a chance. Using them regularly will lower your food expenses.

2. Plant a Garden

Gardening vegetables is a great hobby that you can even make a profit on. Choose veggies that are abundant and easily grown, like tomatoes. (OK, we know that the tomato is actually a fruit, but bear with us.) Learn to can (store) your excess vegetables so you can eat them any time of year. Using foods you store yourself will trim your food bill.

3. Buy Non-perishable Food Items in Bulk

Although it doesn't always save money, some foods bought in bulk will cut your expenses. Look at the cost per serving on the grocery shelf labels. Get the best deals. Look for coupons or coupon codes for foods you use a lot. Don't buy foods your family doesn't like, even if they are on sale.

When you buy in bulk and use coupons, the amount you save on non-perishables like health and beauty products and foods can really add up.

4. Cut Back on Eating Out

Dining out and grabbing food in drive-through fast food restaurants saves time, but costs more money than preparing meals at home. Check out options like preparing meals in advance and freezing them. Use simple recipes that your family likes.

5. Prepare and Pack Meals at Home

If you prepare meals at home, make extra and put some aside for future meals and leftovers to take to work. Stick to recipes that store well, so that everyone will be happy with eating leftovers for lunch.

Lowering your Energy Bills

From cold winters to hot summers and with all

the electronics you have today, you probably spend a lot of your monthly income on energy. There are some effective ways you can improve the energy efficiency of your home and lower those bills, though.

1. Lower your Hot Water Heater Temperature

Keeping a large tank full of water hot accounts for more than 10% of your household energy costs. Your water may be kept even hotter than you need it, and the heat is lost constantly. This means more energy must be burned to keep the water hot.

You can solve both these problems by dropping down your water heater temperature. Install a blanket on your water heater, to keep the heat in. Insulate pipes that are exposed, to save more. Consider installing point-of-contact heaters, which heat only the water you need, only when you need it.

2. Use Power Strips and Timers

Use power timers and power strips to turn your electrical devices off and on. Power strips will block phantom charging of the devices plugged into it. Timers can turn off power at certain times of day.

3. Unplug Electrical Devices when not being Used

Do you have devices plugged in all the time, even when you're not using them? They probably draw small amounts of electricity constantly. That adds up. Unplug power strips or devices you aren't using.

4. Install Programmable Thermostats

Programmable thermostats allow you to change the cooling and heating of your house when you're not there and when you're sleeping. This saves you a lot on air conditioning and heating bills. You can set them to cool or heat your house right before you get home from your job, too.

5. Install LED or CFL Light Bulbs

If you haven't updated the bulbs in your house, switch them out for LEDs or CFLs. These are roughly four times more efficient than conventional bulbs, and they last for years. Even if you only swap out the bulbs you use most often, this could save you more than $40 per year on electric bills.

These tips will help you to reduce your expenses, freeing up more money to pay down that debt.

Chapter 10

Follow the 3 M's –
Make More Money

One of the most logical ways to get out of debt is by making more money, so you can pay more on your debts each month. You can find a second job at a local business, but many people choose to work online to make more money. You can sometimes work whenever you have time when you work online, and you won't be away from home all the time.

There are some legitimate ways you can many money online. None of them are the types of schemes that promise you will get rich quick. Most online jobs demand work and dedication before you'll see a good paycheck. If you really want to work from home, though, or turn your ideas into a business, it can be done.

Blogging for Profit

Building a profitable blog of your own doesn't take rocket science. It isn't as complicated or expensive as you might think, and the returns can be rewarding.

You'll need three things in order to start your own paying blog:

- A domain

- Domain hosting

- Design

A blog doesn't have to have a slick, expensive look for people to read it. If you become an expert in one area online and provide advice on social media sites, people will visit your blog to get their questions answered.

Domain names are not as expensive as they used to be. It's simply the dot com address of your blog. They are usually $10 or less. You can alternately use WordPress, which is a very popular platform for blogs.

You'll also need hosting for your blog. Some

host owners sell newer customers packages that can be quite expensive. Hosting doesn't have to be expensive. At HostGator, for example, you can buy a year of hosting your site for less than $100.

Lastly, you'll need a good website design. Select a high quality template from various online marketplaces. You don't need to spend a lot of money up-front for web design, but once you start getting more visitors, you may want to spend a bit more, to have a more designed theme.

Writing for Markets Online

Writing for businesses online has gotten a bad reputation. This is in some way due to content mills that pay low-dollar fees for writing. If you know where to look and you're a good writer, you don't have to write for peanuts.

There are literally thousands of opportunities for writing freelancers, and many do pay well. You just need to know the best markets and deliver quality writing that works for the people who purchase it. After you gain your first assignments, you can grow them into relationships that help you keep money flowing in from your work.

Web-based publications are on the increase, and so are print publications that also publish content online. In addition, any business that has a website needs content. Many small companies, corporations and non-profit groups use web-savvy writers to appeal to their consumers.

When you vet the writing market, the pay rate shouldn't be judged solely on the dollar amount. Every writer has his or her own criteria and expectations from a working relationship. Focus on the hourly rate and what is also offered in your writing assignments. This includes payment history, rights and rate. Make sure that you understand what is required of you to complete assignments.

Self-Publishing

Average writers are making money by selling books at both high and low prices. The most important thing is enabling your book to be discovered by people searching for something to read.

Price your books low enough that they could be considered bargains, when you are first setting out.

How does a virtually unknown writer do this in an effective way?

Pricing is important, and dynamic pricing helps to sell books. Start with a low price and advertise your book until it hits a peak in sales charts. Then the price can be raised, to take full advantage of increased visibility.

Readers won't buy your book just because the price is low. The marketplace today has so many books from which readers can choose. The books with the highest quality will rise according to their individual merits, as long as people can find them.

Even though there is lots of competition, focus on quality before you worry about pricing. You can then use trial and error to determine the right price point.

Chapter 11

Paying off Debt –
Pay more than the Minimum
each Month

At the end of the month, when you open your credit card bill, check for the smallest number there. It's the minimum payment due. This is the least you can pay and still avoid late fees while you keep your FICO score intact. You can also pay more than that minimum amount, whenever you are able to. There are solid reasons to do this.

1. You'll remain on the good side of your creditors.

The bank that issued your loan or credit card did it because they felt you were a good credit risk. Based on your credit record at the time of the loan, they were confident that you would pay them back in full. If you max out your card by using it and not paying enough on it, this will damage your credit. They may close out your account.

You don't have to worry a lot about a creditor closing your account, as long as you make at least the minimum payment. If you pay more than the minimum, your debt will disappear more quickly. In addition, paying more than your minimum due will show your creditor that you are committed to reducing your overall debt.

2. You will avoid the maxing out of your card.

If you max out your card, it will damage your credit and also your credibility. Maxing out a card hurts your credit score, driving up your ratio of credit utilization. Maxed out cards look bad on your credit report when you need to get a loan. They show that you are not handling your current credit carefully.

3. You will reduce your ratio of credit utilization.

This ratio is the amount you owe compared to the credit limit. If your total balance is more than 1/3 of the available credit, this will usually lower your credit score. If you can still get credit in the future, it will be at a higher rate of interest, if you need a car loan or a mortgage. Low credit scores can even keep you out of apartments, since some apartment management companies make decisions about potential tenants based on credit scores.

Paying more than the minimum on credit cards and other debts will help in chipping away at the balances on those debts. This will raise your credit score, and eventually leave you with more disposable income. If you still use credit cards for purchases, paying more than the minimum amount due keeps the debt from piling up. Paying at least as much as you charge each month will help in continuously lowering your debt.

The Bottom Line?

With credit cards and other debts, priorities are the key. Make payments on time, and pay more than the minimum amount whenever you can. If you can get to a point where you don't carry a balance on your card, this will help your credit score and your financial health, too.

Tips for Getting out of Debt

Make more money. That seems logical, doesn't it? If you can take on a second job for awhile, that will certainly help you pay off your debts more quickly, since you'll be making larger payments. Working online, as we discussed in chapter 11, is one way to make extra money without ever leaving your home.

Make payments bi-weekly instead of monthly. This will bring your balances down more swiftly, and save you money on interest.

Set up automatic payments. When you have automatic transfers taken from your bank account to make your payments on loans, credit cards or lines of credit, it ensures that your bills will be paid on time and on a regular basis. When you rely solely on your memory to make payments against your debt, you always have the chance to make excuses and spend some of that money on something you want.

Try negotiating the interest rates on your loans. Finance companies and banks are not all cold-hearted and greedy. Some are more willing to work together with you, to pay down your debt. If you have lost your job or for some other reason you are in a period of financial hardship, give your bank a call. You can ask for a lowering of your interest rate, and they just might be willing to help.

These tips will be quite helpful if you are comfortable using "do-it-yourself" methods of paying off debt more quickly. If your debt overwhelms you, there may be a need for you to speak with a debt counselor, as we mentioned in the first chapter. As long as you choose a legitimate debt counseling service, they can be helpful in evaluating your situation and helping you to work on a budget that will allow you to pay off your debt more quickly. You'll feel the weight of the world fall from your shoulders when you are debt-free.

Chapter 12

Know where your Money Goes
—
Record your Spending

The only way you'll know where your money goes is to take the time to track it. The downside to this is that the answers might scare you. You probably spend a lot more money on incidental things than you realize. But once you're aware of this, you can watch your spending more closely.

When you first start recording your spending, it may give you some unwelcome surprises. You may spend more in several categories like eating out, or in most categories across the board. Recording spending habits will help you get on top of your spending and create a less depressing picture.

Make the Changes Needed

The severity of your unrecorded spending may

force you to change, and that's a good thing. Tracking the ways in which you spend your money makes you take a long hard look at where your money goes and what you really spend it on. Your failure to watch your spending in the past is just the wake-up call you need to get on the right track. Use the information you find to track expenses, and transform your life by paying off your debt. It will mean a brighter future for you.

Some people have to hit the bottom financially in order to turn things around. You don't have to wait until things are that bad. When you record your spending, you'll be compelled to take action. You have to want to make the change, though. When you do, you'll be glad not to have to worry about your finances all the time.

Tracking your Spending and why you should do it

If you want to know the full story of your financial situation, tracking your spending will be a great start. You may believe that you only spend $X every month for transportation and groceries, for example, but what are you really spending? Record that spending and you won't have to wonder anymore.

Commit to using the records of your spending to help your cause. No one will do this for you. You may be in for an eye-opening experience, and you'll need your family's cooperation. Once you decide to record your spending, don't do it half-way. Record everything, so you know where you need to cut back.

Track Online Spending

Keeping track of money you spend locally is often easier than tracking what you spend online. But you need to know what you spend online, too. This may include online bill-paying, shopping and debit and credit card transactions. Email yourself a copy of the order confirmation for purchases made or bills paid online so you'll have them. If you need to print them out to have them handy, that's fine, too. You want a complete picture of all the money you and your family spend, so you need to include each transaction during the month.

Keep your Receipts

Yes, even little stops to pick up just a few things should be recorded. You need all your receipts for the month. This is a hassle, particularly if you don't usually do it. But it's essential to the process, so it needs to be done.

Total the Receipts

At the end of your trial month, tally up everything. Gather your online transactions and receipts and total them. Lump similar categories together, so that they are easier to track. Categories vary from one person to the next, but they will usually include, among others, home maintenance, hobbies, medical bills, clothing, gas, eating out and groceries.

Be Honest in your Recording

If you faithfully track all your spending for the month and the results shock you, don't make excuses for the excess money spent. Learn from your mistakes. Otherwise, you'll just go back to the way you've been living, which has been adding to your debt, possibly for years. That road doesn't lead anywhere good. It's actually easier to record the spending than to face the facts you turn up. That's harder.

You have to recognize what you're spending and on what items before you can change. And until you change, you won't have the funds to make much of a dent in your debts. If you don't understand the problem, you won't be able to tackle it. Recording your spending habits may be the worst part of your journey out of debt. It's also the most important step.

There's No one to Blame but Yourself

Once you have seen your spending totals, you can't blame your schedule or the rest of the family. You may still need a raise at work, but that's not the reason you don't have money to pay down your debt. It's probably because you spend too much on things you never kept track of before.

People create their own types of prison cells, whether it's due to laziness or from force of habit. When you do this, it's too easy to blame others and feel that it's impossible to escape the hole you've dug for yourself. Recording spending is vital to getting out of debt. It brings you face to face with the most urgent threat to your future.

Here are some little tips you can keep in mind that will give you a step toward getting rid of your debt:

1. Pay off your credit cards as soon as you can, along with other high interest debts or loans.

2. Never keep more than one or two credit cards. If you have more than that, cancel the extras.

3. Research what you need to purchase before you buy and comparison shop for the best prices.

4. If you want something you cannot afford, don't put it on a charge card unless it is an actual emergency.

5. Put a percentage of each paycheck into savings instead of checking. You won't be as likely to spend the money if you don't see it.

6. Save money for something you need and then purchase it. Set aside a few dollars every day or

every week until you have the money to buy it.

7.   Break a small – or large – habit, like buying lottery tickets or drinking soda, smoking or chewing gum. Save the money you used to spend on them.

8.   Keep your eyes open for loose change and toss it in a jar to save it.

9.   Put away and save money you save with coupons.

Chapter 13

Set Targets and Work Hard to Meet them

When you set targets, they give you a chance to take more control of your debt and your money. These goals may be over the long term or short term, and large or small, but they must be goals you can achieve. The first step is working out what you want your financial future to look like, and in setting up priorities.

Setting Goals

Be realistic and specific. Write down all your goals. Make sure they are simple, and easily tracked. Give them a dollar amount and a time frame.

Set some larger goals, like perhaps purchasing a house in the next 10 years, or saving more for your retirement.

Set a few smaller goals that will help in keeping

you motivated as you meet them. These may include paying off a credit card or saving for a large ticket item that you need.

Saving Money and Paying down your Debt

Financial goals often are related to savings or to paying down your debt. If you have debts that carry high interest rates, pay those off as soon as you can. You may be able to restructure high-interest debt into a lower-interest loan.

Saving money for several months and establishing an emergency fund with it will help you if something unexpected happens in your life. Put this money in a separate savings account, away from the accounts you use every day.

If your home is mortgaged, increase your payments if you can afford to do this. It will save you money on interest, since you'll be paying your loan off sooner.

The sooner you begin saving for retirement, the better off you'll be. Even small amounts set aside each week or each month can add up, over the years.

Taking Steps to Reach Goals

Actions are steps taken to reach financial goals. Some examples include:

If you pay monthly on your mortgage, your goal can be to change that to bi-weekly payments of one half or more of their original amounts. This pays off your mortgage more quickly and saves money on interest you would otherwise pay.

If you're saving up to make a down payment on a house, open a new savings account by the end of THIS month and put $50 or more into that account each week.

Reviewing your Goals

Stop and review the progress you have made every six or 12 months, on a date you note on your calendar. Celebrate as you achieve goals and then set new ones. When New Years Day rolls around, write down your resolutions as goals, if they are achievable.

Using your Goals Worksheet

Writing down your goals and taking the time to review them on a regular basis means you will be more likely to ultimately achieve those goals.

A worksheet for goals makes setting goals easy. Jot down long, short and medium-term goals and save the worksheets, to review as needed. Worksheets also allow you to set actions that will help in achieving your goals.

One of your long-term goals should be digging yourself out of debt. Every dollar above the minimum payment you pay each month on high interest debts will help you to meet this goal.

Conclusion

This e-book has given you all the ammunition you need for a war against debt. It's time to decide that enough is enough. Your debt-filled lifestyle was not working, and you were ready to make some changes.

We taught you to be wise, so that you knew where your income should be going, and patient, since paying off debt can't happen overnight. We gave you the tools to become goal-driven and confident in your ability to leave debt behind.

You're more responsible now, too. You have to be mature to treat money in a way that decreases debt. You have learned not to be materialistic, and only to buy the things you really need. You are willing now to make sacrifices where they are needed.

You are motivated now to get out of debt for good. Get out there and become debt-free!

www.ingramcontent.com/pod-product-compliance
Lightning Source LLC
Chambersburg PA
CBHW071804170526
45167CB00003B/1170